The Christmas Shoppe

An Advent Experience for Children

Daphna Flegal and Marcia Stoner

Abingdon Press
Nashville

MARCIA STONER has worked with tweens and youth for over thirty years. She is currently an editor of tween curriculum for The United Methodist Publishing House. Marcia is the writer of *Symbols of Faith* and *What Is Advent?* among other books.

DAPHNA FLEGAL is a diaconal minister in The United Methodist Church. She has worked with preschool children for more than twenty years. Daphna is currently the lead editor for children's curriculum. She is the writer of *On the Way to Bethlehem* and *Sign & Say Bible Verses for Children*, among other books.

ISBN: 978-142674295-8

PACP 01010494-01

Editor: Daphna Flegal
Production Editor: Norma Bates
Designers: Kellie Green and Kent Sneed
Photos: Paige Easter and Ron Benedict

12 13 14 15 16 17 18 19 20 21—10 9 8 7 6 5 4 3 2

Printed in the U. S. A.

Contents

CD-ROM Contents

Bible Story Scripts
  (one for each Department)
  Legend of the Candy Cane

Craft Directions
  Angel Department
  Manger Department
  Candy Cane Department
  Star Department
  Card Department
  Bakery Department

Directions for Department Heads

Forms

Patterns and Tags

Supply Lists

Worship PowerPoint®
  Music With Words (to be used with closing worship)

Worship Scripts
  Worship Outline
  Worship Scripts (one for each Department)

Introduction

Welcome to *The Christmas Shoppe*.

Leave behind your preconceptions of a Christmas shop as a place to buy things you don't really need. This is a Christmas shop with a real difference. It is Christ-centered and shopping is not the point.

The Christmas Shoppe is an event where children of all ages will hear the Christmas story, create Christmas symbols to be sold to support a mission project of the church's choice, and prepare and participate in a worship service with parents or with the entire congregation.

You may choose from different options as to how to proceed with your event. Here are some suggested options:

1. A large one-day event, ending with a worship service and a fund-raiser sale. See page 8 for a schedule.
2. A Saturday evening, Sunday morning event with children leading a worship experience, followed by a fund-raiser sale. See top of page 9 for a schedule.
3. A four-week Advent Study with or without a separate worship and/or fund-raiser sale. See bottom of page 9 for a schedule.

The Christmas Shoppe is experienced through six "shops" or departments. The four symbol departments tell the part of the Christmas story that goes with their symbol. The symbols are the angel, the manger, the candy cane, and the star. The Card Department will talk about the spreading of the good news of the birth of the Savior. The Bakery Department will use Isaiah 9:2–6 as the basis for its part of the Christmas theme.

Within the time in each department, children will hear part of the Christmas story and make items for the sale.

The second portion of the event deals with preparing for a closing worship presentation and setting up for the sale itself. We encourage you to make the closing worship presentation and the sale open to the entire congregation.

If you should choose to do only four of the departments, you will need to do the four symbol departments to create the entire biblical story for your children.

The CD-ROM provides music, PowerPoints®, and scripts to be used to produce the worship experience. Scripts for Bible stories and the patterns for crafts are provided both in the book and on the CD-ROM for your convenience.

Tips for the Director

Setup and recruiting can be extensive if you will have a large number attending this event. However, these plans allow you to "think outside the box" when recruiting.

Recruiting Volunteers

Craft people and bakers—Are there people in your church who don't ordinarily teach but have the gift of crafting or of baking? They make wonderful volunteers. Older adults might indeed be flattered to be asked to help children in this special way on a one–time basis.

Setup and cleanup—Tweens and teens are great at making signs and could do this in advance. Ask the youth group to help set up for the event as a service to the children of the church. If asked ahead of time, adult Sunday school classes might be willing to help with setup and cleanup. Is there someone who does not like to teach but loves to throw parties (especially theme parties)? That person would be a real help in decorating for the event.

Deciding on the Mission Project

Many churches have many missions they support, especially going into the holiday season. Adding a new mission project may not be feasible at this time. Coordinate with your missions committee to determine which mission might be most appropriate for your children to participate in. Church buy-in to the mission project and the entire project is vital.

Advertising

Advertising is critical if this is to be a large event with a sale. You will need to advertise both to children and to those who will be attending the sale.

The Christmas Shoppe as a Study

The Christmas Shoppe can be done as a four-week study. It can be done with any number of children. If a sale is just not an option for you, choose some deserving people in your church or local community who might appreciate receiving cards or ornaments and have the children hand-deliver these as gifts.

Further Information

For forms, shopping lists, and advertising helps, you will want to look at the "Forms and Other Useful Information" section at the back of this book (page 87).

Mission Project Introduction

Most churches have special mission projects that take on real significance during the Advent/Christmas season. This year give your children an opportunity to actively participate in one of these missions.

Choose a mission to which money is usually donated. During *The Christmas Shoppe* event have children create symbolic ornaments to sell. Let the children set up the sale and do the selling. Be sure that they are the ones who turn over the money, either to the church or to the chosen mission.

Some possible mission projects:
- Homeless Shelter
- Angel Tree (Money could be used to purchase items asked for.)
- A Manger Project
- Disaster Relief
- Food Bank
- National or International Mission Project sponsored by your church or denomination
- Any program for disadvantaged children or youth
- A Children's Hospital (Many will be glad to have donations for books and toys for sick children.)

Option: Instead of choosing a project for which you raise money, you may instead opt to forgo the sale. You may wish to choose a project such as people in nursing homes. The children make the ornaments and deliver them to the residents.

Whatever project you choose, be sure to check with the agency involved before beginning.

Schedule/One-Day Event

Note: Five-minute intervals are given for changing departments.

Time	Activity
9:00– 9:15	Registration and Assigning of Department Rotation
9:15– 9:20	Opening Advent Wreath Worship
9:20– 9:45	First Department
9:50–10:15	Second Department
10:15–10:25	Break within department (Small snack may be served at this time.)
10:30 – 10:55	Third Department
11:00 –11:25	Fourth Department
11:30 – 12:10	LUNCH
12:10–12:35	Fifth Department
12:40– 1:10	Sixth Department (The last five minutes in this department are to be used to explain the closing worship.)
1:10 – 1:30	By department groups, everyone is to gather in the area for closing worship for a quick run-through of their participation.
1:30 – 2:45	Set up for sale and Closing Worship

Immediately following Closing Worship: CHRISTMAS SHOPPE SALE

The Christmas Shoppe

Schedule/Weekend Event

Saturday Afternoon

Note: Department times will overlap. Each child will go to three departments.

Time	Activity
1:00–1:15	Registration and Assigning of Department Rotation
1:20– 1:25	Advent Worship
1:25–1:50	First Department
1:55–2:20	Second Department
2:25–3:00	Third Department (ten-minute break to be taken in this department.)
3:00–3:30	Go by third department groupings to worship area and run through assignments and flow of worship service.
3:30–4:30	Set up for sale

Sunday Morning
Worship service followed by Christmas Shoppe Sale.

Schedule/Four-Week Event
Each week, begin with the appropriate Advent Wreath Lighting.
Week 1:   Angel and Manger Departments
Week 2:   Candy and Star Departments
Week 3:   Card Department and Bakery
Week 4:   Prepare for worship and sale (to be held at time determined by you).

Room Setup

If you have a large fellowship hall or gym close to a kitchen, you may wish to use this possible setup for your event. Place a large banner over the entrance, labeled "The Christmas Shoppe." Place your registration table in the hallway outside the entrance. Place a sign or banner on (or over) each table representing each "Department." Place a rug near each table for storytelling time. Or each department might be in a separate room in one wing of the church.

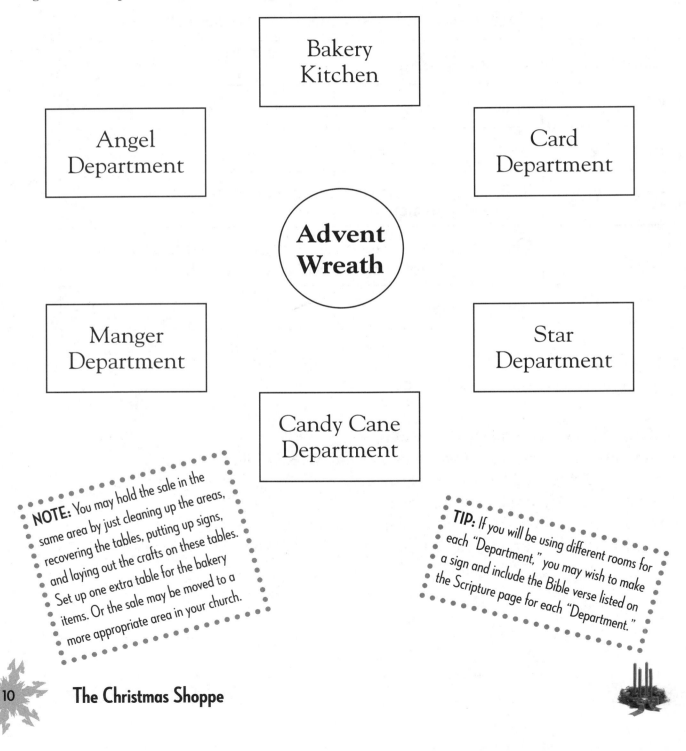

Bakery Kitchen

Angel Department

Card Department

Advent Wreath

Manger Department

Star Department

Candy Cane Department

NOTE: You may hold the sale in the same area by just cleaning up the areas, recovering the tables, putting up signs, and laying out the crafts on these tables. Set up one extra table for the bakery items. Or the sale may be moved to a more appropriate area in your church.

TIP: If you will be using different rooms for each "Department," you may wish to make a sign and include the Bible verse listed on the Scripture page for each "Department."

Grand Opening

The Christmas Shoppe

Registration

- As families arrive, have parents register their children. (Preregistration is encouraged as it will help you with planning and with purchasing the appropriate number of supplies.)

- If children have been preregistered, check their names as they arrive. Direct children to the table where they will decorate bags.

You will need:
registration forms
index cards with department order

Decorate Bags (optional)

- Have the children go immediately from registration to a table with the bags and decorating supplies laid out.

- Explain that they will be decorating bags in which to place items sold during the sale.

- Encourage creativity and stress quick production.

- If you have not done so ahead of time, ask for tween or older elementary volunteers to read Scripture and light Advent candles.

You will need:
small brown or white lunch bags
or
plain, inexpensive gift bags
stickers
markers
ribbon
tape
scissors

NOTE: You will probably not have time for all bags to be decorated. Plain plastic bags saved from stores may be used as backup.

Advent Wreath Worship

- At the appointed time gather everyone around the Advent wreath in the center of the "Christmas Shoppe."

- If you are doing the one-day event or the Saturday evening, Sunday morning event, use the Advent Worship on page 14.

- If you are doing a four-week Advent Study, use the individual Advent Wreath Lighting worships on pages 15–16 (one per week)

Advent Worship

Ahead of time choose four children to light the Advent candles and give them instructions.

You will need:
Advent wreath with four purple or blue candles
butane lighter

NOTE: If you have time, you may wish to add the song "Let's Get Ready, A Savior's Coming" to this Advent Worship. It is the first song on your CD-ROM.

- Have children gather around the Advent wreath for opening worship.

SAY: Because we are meeting only this one time before Christmas, we are going to light all four candles on the Advent wreath. The lighting of the Advent wreath helps prepare our hearts for the birth of Jesus, our Savior.

SAY: We light the first candle as a symbol of Christ who brings Hope.

- Have a child light the first candle.

SAY: We light the second candle as a symbol of Christ who brings Joy.

- Have a child light the second candle.

SAY: We light the third candle as a symbol of Christ who brings Love.

- Have a child light the third candle.

SAY: We light the fourth candle as a symbol of Christ, the Prince of Peace.

- Have a child light the fourth candle.

SAY: Because the birth of Jesus, the Christ brings us hope, joy, love, and peace, we want to share these with others.

- Explain your mission project and why it was chosen.

- Tell the children that they will be making crafts to sell to donate to this mission.

- Explain the day's schedule.

PRAY: God, we come today filled with hope, joy, love, and peace. We ask your blessing upon us and our mission. In Jesus' name we pray. Amen.

- Dismiss children to their first Department, checking to be sure they go to the assigned Department.

TIP: If laws in your community do not allow the use of candles in public places, you can substitute LED candles instead.

Advent Wreath Lighting for Weekly Sessions

Each week ask different children to light the Advent Candle and read Scripture.

Begin each session with children decorating bags for the sale (arrival time only, see page 13). Then have everyone come together for the Advent Wreath Lighting as opening worship.

Week One

SAY: We light the first candle as a symbol of Christ who brings Hope.

- Ask an older elementary child to read Isaiah 60:1.

- Have a child light the first candle.

PRAY: Our God, we come to you today filled with hope. We ask your blessing upon us and our mission. In Jesus' name we pray. Amen.

- Explain your chosen mission project and why it was chosen.

- Tell the children that they will be making crafts over the next three weeks to sell to make money to donate to this mission.

You will need:
Bible
Advent wreath with four purple or blue candles
butane lighter

Week Two

SAY: We light the first candle as a symbol of Christ who brings Hope.

- Have a child light the first candle.

SAY: We light the second candle as a symbol of Christ who brings Joy.

- Have a child read Isaiah 12:6.

- Have a child light the second candle.

PRAY: Our God, we come to you today filled with joy. Help us work joyfully today. In Jesus' name we pray. Amen.

Week Three

SAY: We light the first candle as a symbol of Christ who brings Hope.

- Have a child light the first candle.

SAY: We light the second candle as a symbol of Christ who brings Joy.

- Have a child light the second candle.

SAY: We light the third candle as a symbol of Christ who brings Love.

- Have a child read John 3:16.

- Have a child light the third candle.

PRAY: Our God, we come to you today filed with love. Help us work together in a loving way today. In Jesus' name we pray. Amen.

• •

Week Four

SAY: We light the first candle as a symbol of Christ who brings Hope.

- Have a child light the first candle.

SAY: We light the second candle as a symbol of Christ who brings Joy.

- Have a child light the second candle.

SAY: We light the third candle as a symbol of Christ who brings Love.

- Have a child light the third candle.

SAY: We light the fourth candle as a symbol of Christ, the Prince of Peace.

- Have a child read Isaiah 9:6.

- Have a child light the fourth candle.

PRAY: Our God, we come to you today in the spirit of peace. Help us work together peacefully today. In Jesus' name we pray. Amen.

Angel Department

Matthew 1:18-24
and
Luke 1:26-38

The angel, Gabriel, announces the coming birth of Jesus to Joseph and Mary.

"The angel said, 'Don't be afraid, Mary. God is honoring you. Look! You will conceive and give birth to a son, and you will name him Jesus.'" (Luke 1:30)

Directions for Angel Department

The head of the Angel Department will be responsible for organizing the setup of the department prior to the event. The Department Head will also be responsible for the overall supervision of the department during the event.

The Angel Department Head checklist:

❏ Bible storyteller lined up and prepared.

❏ Angel crafts chosen and all directions and supplies on hand.

❏ Make sure that one sample of each craft is on hand for display.

❏ Supplies laid out by craft (preferably one per table, or end of a long table).

❏ Department Helpers have instructions and know exactly how to do the craft they are helping with. (Or if only one helper, that the helper is familiar with all the crafts.)

❏ Check that children are in the correct department.

> **TIP:** Crafts are listed by abilities rather than ages, because abilities do not necessarily relate directly to age. While guiding younger children to easy-to-manipulate crafts, allow older children some leeway in which angel they think they can do well.

DEPARTMENT SESSION OUTLINE

- Children checked as they arrive to ensure they are in the correct department.
- All children sit and storyteller is introduced.
- Storyteller tells story.
- Children directed to appropriate crafts.
- Children make chosen angels until time to move to next department or until close of session.

Possible crafts for the Angel Department:

EASY:
Lollipop angel

MEDIUM:
Paper Clip Angel
Pencil Angel (optional)

ADVANCED:
Beaded Angel
Yarn Angel (optional)

Bible Story Script

(Hold a cell phone in one hand as you begin talking.)

Welcome to the Angel Department. I hope you find it just heavenly! My name is Angelica (or Angelo) and I'm in charge of all the angels here at The Christmas Shoppe. Oh, excuse me just a minute—I'm getting a message. *(Look at cell phone as if you are reading a text message; then pretend to text a reply.)* Sorry. Um. What was I saying? Oh yes, yes. I remember. My name is Angelica (or Angelo) and I'm in charge of all the angels here at The Christmas Shoppe. Today I'm going to tell you something very important. Whoops! I'm getting another message—I'll just be a minute. *(Look at cell phone as if you are reading a text message; then pretend to text a reply.)* Sorry. Um. What was I saying? Oh yes. I remember. My name is Angelica (or Angelo) and I'm in charge of all the angels here at The Christmas Shoppe. Oh. I guess I said that already didn't I? Yes. Well. I have something really important to tell you. Um. Hold on. It's another message! I keep getting messages and I want to answer them but I also want to tell you something important. What should I do? *(Let the children make suggestions.)* Turn off my phone? Oh. Okay. *(Pretend to turn off phone.)* Good thinking.

Alright. Let me start again. My name is Angelica (or Angelo) and I'm in charge of all the angels here at The Christmas Shoppe. I know I keep getting a lot of messages, but I have a good reason for that. Angels are messengers. That's right. We are messengers from God. And boy, do I have an important message for you. Here it is: God loves you! Wow! That's huge! That's amazing! In fact, that may be the most important message you will ever hear. God loves you! God. Loves. You. And you know what? This is a message you can share with your friends and family, because God loves them too.

I remember when the angel Gabriel delivered two really important messages for God. First, Gabriel went to a young woman named Mary. Do you know what he told her? *(Pause for children to respond.)* He told her that God had chosen her to be the mother of God's Son. Wow! What an honor.

Then Gabriel visited Joseph in a dream. Gabriel told Joseph that Mary's baby was God's Son and that Joseph should go ahead with his marriage to Mary. Then Gabriel told Joseph to name the baby Jesus. And do you know what Mary and Joseph did? Exactly what Gabriel told them to do. Mary and Joseph were married and when Mary gave birth to her baby boy, they named him Jesus.

And do you know why God sent Jesus as a newborn baby? Because God loves you!

The Christmas Shoppe

Lollipop Angel

- Place a lollipop in the center of a square of fabric.

- Cover the "ball" of the lollipop.

- Tie a ribbon in a knot at the base of the ball to create the angel's head.

- Use a fine-tip marker to draw a face on the fabric head.

- Glue hair to the top of the angel's head.

- Tie the one-inch ribbon in a bow (or pretied bows may be used).

- Attach bow to the back of the angel, using the safety pin.

TIP: If older children choose to do this angel, have some extra ribbon available and let them cut, staple, and curl ribbon (under supervision.)

You will need:
light-colored fabric
chocolate-filled, fruit-flavored lollipops
curling ribbon (red, white, brown, yellow, or gold)
1-inch ribbons, about 18 inches in length
safety pins
fine-tip felt markers
stapler and staples
scissors
glue

AHEAD OF TIME:

Cut cloth into five-inch squares.

Cut curling ribbon in pieces approximately 18 inches long and staple them in the center.
Use tip of scissors to curl the ribbon.

Paper Clip Angel

TIP: You may wish to add a tiny dot of glue to the beads to hold them in place.

- Cut ribbon in lengths long enough to hang the ornament from a tree.

- Tie a loop in the ribbon.

- Thread a flat bead and then a pony bead onto the ribbon.

- Push the bead and the disk up to the knot on the ribbon.

- Thread the ribbon through the paperclip clamp

- Slide two beads onto each side of the clamp for further decoration. You will definitely want to add a drop of glue to the bottom bead on each side to make sure they stay on the angel.

- You may wish to add a small, ready-made rose to the center of the angel. To do this, wrap the stem of the rose around the middle of the clip and trim off any excess.

NOTE: A rose is the symbol of prophecy. It is the symbol for Isaiah who prophesied the coming of the Messiah.

Pencil Angel

- Roll one coffee filter into a tight ball. This forms a head.

- Place the ball in the center of the remaining coffee filters.

- Gather the filters and twist around the ball.

- Cut chenille stems two inches in length.

- Twist a two-inch length of the chenille stem around the coffee filters to form a neck.

- Place the filters over a pencil's eraser end, loosening the chenille stem at the neck in order to push the pencil through it.

- Twist the chenille stem tightly in order to hold the pencil. (A touch of glue on the eraser before pushing it through will help secure the pencil in place.)

- Decorate the "dress" of the angel with a fine-tip marker. Use a fine-tip marker if you wish to give the angel a "face."

- Shape one chenille stem into a figure 8 and glue it to the back of the angel. Shape into wings.

- Form a small piece of chenille stem into a circle and glue onto the angel's head (or tie the halo to the wings to avoid using glue).

- Form a piece of chenille stem into a loop and glue it to the back of the angel for a hanger.

You will need:
unsharpened pencils
chenille stems
construction paper
5 coffee filters per angel
scissors
fine-tip markers
glue

TIP: If you construct the wings first you can tie them to make angel's head and you won't have to glue.

Beaded Angel

For each angel you will need:
two beads, one larger than the other

¼-inch wire-edged ribbon

thick thread (such as quilting thread or jewelry wire)

scissors

- Cut a 22-inch strip of wire-edged ribbon to make the wings.

- Fold the ribbon in an accordion fold, making three folded loops on each side for angel wings.

- Tie the wings in the center.

- Cut the two ends of the ribbon where they just pass the middle point.

- Thread the thread or wire through the larger bead bringing both ends up equal, one on each side, to the top center of the bead. (This makes the body.)

- Knot the thread on the top center of the bead.

- Place wings on top of the knot and tie the thread (or wire) again on top of the wings. This ties the wings to the body. Make sure this knot is secure. (A little bit of glue might help at this point.)

- Thread both ends of the string (or wire) through the smaller bead (head) and tie a knot to secure it in place.

- Tie a knot in the top of the two ends of the wire to make the extra string (or wire) into a hanger.

- Unfold the ribbon wings.

Yarn Angel

- Cut a 28½-inch piece of yarn and a 6-by-3-inch piece of cardboard. The yarn will be wrapped around the cardboard twenty-eight times, so the yarn needs to be very long. (Can be trimmed off with a pair of scissors.)

- Wrap the yarn lengthwise around the cardboard twenty–eight times.

- Measure and cut a twelve-inch piece of yarn, a four-inch piece of yarn, and a four-inch piece of yarn. (You may do this step in advance to save time.)

- Very carefully take the yarn off the cardboard.

- Tie the twelve-inch piece of yarn around the middle of the wrapped yarn. (This piece of yarn becomes the hanger.)

- Fold the yarn bundle in half and tie off a section for the head using a four-inch piece of yarn.

- Separate six or seven strands of yarn on each side of the body. These sections will be arms. Bring the two "arms" to the front of the body, letting them meet in front. Make wrists by tying the end of the arms together with a four-inch piece of yarn.

- Make a waist for the angel by tying a six-inch piece of gold cord around the middle of the body. Trim off any excess.

- Bend a 3½-inch piece of gold tinsel stem into a circle to make a halo. Glue the halo on the angel's head.

- Fold a four-inch doily in half and crease it. Glue the doily onto the angel to make wings.

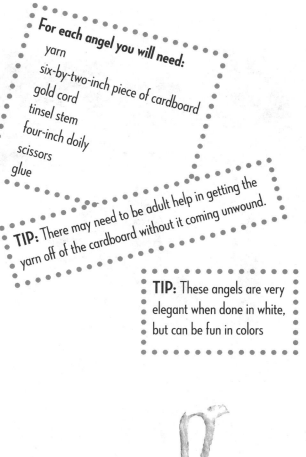

For each angel you will need:
yarn
six-by-two-inch piece of cardboard
gold cord
tinsel stem
four-inch doily
scissors
glue

TIP: There may need to be adult help in getting the yarn off of the cardboard without it coming unwound.

TIP: These angels are very elegant when done in white, but can be fun in colors

The Christmas Shoppe

Manger Department

Luke 2:1-7

Joseph and Mary go to Bethlehem to be enrolled in the tax lists.

"She gave birth to her firstborn child, a son, wrapped him snugly, and laid him in a manger, because there was no place for them in the guestroom." (Luke 2:7)

Directions for Manger Department

The head of the Manger Department will be responsible for organizing the setup of the department prior to the event. The Department Head will also be responsible for the overall supervision of the department during the event.

The Manger Department Head checklist:

❑ Bible storyteller lined up and prepared.

❑ Nativity and manger crafts chosen and all directions and supplies on hand.

❑ Make sure that one sample of each craft is on hand for display.

❑ Supplies laid out by craft (preferably one per table, or end of a long table).

❑ Department Helpers have instructions and know exactly how to do the craft they are helping with. (Or if only one helper, that the helper is familiar with all the crafts.)

❑ Manger pattern photocopied.

❑ Check that children are in the correct department.

> **TIP:** Crafts are listed by abilities rather than ages, because abilities do not necessarily relate directly to age. While guiding younger children to easy-to-manipulate crafts, allow older children some leeway in which craft they think they can do well.

DEPARTMENT SESSION OUTLINE

- Children checked as they arrive to ensure they are in the correct department.
- All children sit and storyteller is introduced.
- Storyteller tells story.
- Children directed to appropriate crafts.
- Children make chosen nativities/mangers until time to move to next department or until close of session.

Possible crafts for the Manger Department:

EASY:
Mini Clay Pots Nativity

MEDIUM:
Yarn Baby Jesus
"Stone Box" Manger

ADVANCED:
Twig (Stick) Nativity

Bible Story Script

Welcome honored guests! I am so grateful that you stopped by my humble guesthouse. Your room is almost ready, but please, take a few minutes and sit down. Relax. Make yourself comfortable. I, of course, am your innkeeper. (*Bow.*)

The inn is usually full, you are lucky that I have a room for you. I remember a night not so long ago when I would have had to turn you away. All because of the Romans. The emperor, Caesar Augustus, made a law that everyone had to be counted. Of course he just wanted to tax us. Romans, bah! Anyway, the city was bursting with people. There were no rooms anywhere. I had just locked up for the night and was going to my own bed when there was a knock at my door. (*Knock on the table or pretend to knock on a door.*) I stopped at the sound. (*Sigh.*) It must be another weary traveler, I thought, but I had no room. I considered not even answering the knock, but for some reason I turned around and went back to the door. When I opened it there was a young couple. They looked so tired.

"Please," said the man. "Do you have any room? We have made a long journey and my wife is about to have a baby."

What could I do? The guestroom was already taken. Then I had an idea.

"You can stay in the stable," I told the young couple. "It will be dry and warm. You can sleep on the hay."

The young couple gratefully agreed. I led them to the stable and told them good night. And it *was* a good night. An amazing night. For that night the young woman had her baby. She wrapped him in soft cloths so he felt safe and warm. The young man filled the manger, the animals' feeding box with hay. The young woman laid the baby on the soft bed.

Yes, it was an amazing night. You know, for a moment I thought I heard angels singing. But that's impossible, isn't it? It must have been the woman singing her newborn child to sleep.

Mini Clay Pots Nativity

- Paint the pots and the saucer using paint pens.

- Use a marker to draw faces on the wooden knobs.

- Allow paint to dry.

- Turn the pots upside down. Use tacky glue to attach a larger bead to the bottom of each pot for a head.

- Drape a piece of fabric around the top of each head and tie it in place with embroidery floss.

- With a separate piece of cloth form a tightly wrapped blanket by wrapping it around a cotton ball.

- Glue a small knob or bead to the cotton ball to make the head. Glue the head to the blanket in place.

For each Nativity you will need:
2 small pots (terra cotta or plastic)
1 small saucer (terra cotta or plastic)
paint pens
permanent marker
3 wooden knobs or beads (2 larger, 1 smaller)
tacky glue
fabric
embroidery floss
raffia
cotton ball

- Tear raffia and place it in the saucer to make "straw" for the manger.

- Set the baby on the bed of straw.

Yarn Baby Jesus

- To make the body, glue two cotton balls together.

- Wrap a chenille stick around the cotton balls, bottom to top. Twist the chenille stick tightly once. Add one more cotton ball. (This forms the head.) Bring the chenille stem around both sides of the "head," twist the stem and trim it off.

- Tie the center of the "skin-colored" yarn around the neck. Wrap it (in double thickness) up to the head stem and back. (Glue may be used if needed.) Tie it at the "neck."

- Tie one end of the "blanket" yarn around the neck, using glue as needed.

- Wrap yarn around the body.

For each baby Jesus you will need:
chenille stick
ruler
scissors
jumbo cotton balls,
three-to-five-feet of yarn for "skin"
eight-to-ten feet of bulky weight yarn for the "swaddling clothes"
tacky glue
sequins for eyes

- Tie off the yarn at the "neck," trim it, and tuck in the ends.

- The "eyes" can be made by cutting a sequin in half and gluing them in place. (Or use very small sequins.)

NOTE: This baby Jesus goes in the stone box manger.

"Stone Box" Manger

- Trace the manger onto white paper.

- Cut out the manger (cut out the section between the lines for the manger and the top).

- Using markers, color the "wooden" sides and top brown.

- Color the stones different shades of brown (or may use all one shade).

- Color the "mortar" between the stones black or gray.

- Using the small star pattern, cut the star from yellow construction paper and punch a hole as shown.

- Glue the star to the top of the manger. Thread a ribbon through the hole and tie it. This makes a hanger for the manger.

- Fold the manger as shown by the dotted lines on the pattern.

- Glue the sides of the manger together. (Do NOT glue front and back together. This must be open for the Yarn Baby Jesus, see page 32.)

- Gently open the manger in the center.

- Place short pieces of raffia inside.

- Place the Yarn Baby Jesus in the manger.

You will need:
- patterns on page 34
- white paper
- brown and gray or black markers
- yellow construction paper (for star)
- glue
- yarn
- raffia
- scissors
- hole punch

Patterns for "Stone Box" Manger

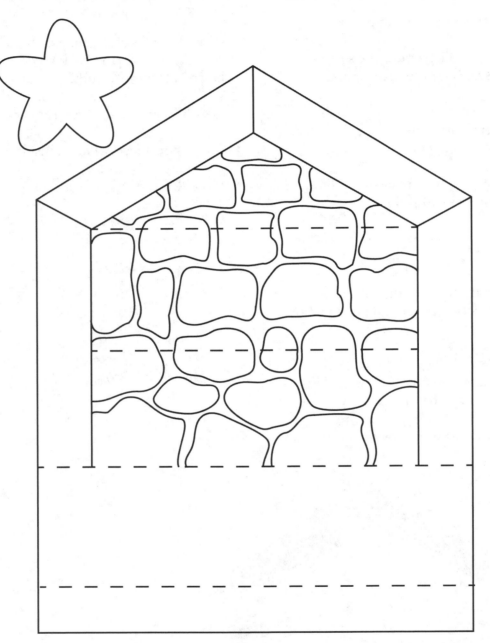

- Cut out the manger.

- Cut along solid line on the inside of the manger to separate the stones from the manger.

- Fold on the dashed lines.

The Christmas Shoppe

Twig (Stick) Nativity

Begin to use the widest twigs or sticks to form a five-sided shape (to make the house). Wire each end of the bundles and each joint with very thin wire.

- Glue one or two more layers of twigs (sticks) around the shape.

- You may wish to use vines to wrap around the twigs.

- Glue dried grass, grains (or raffia) to the bottom of the shape to make hay.

- Make baby Jesus by wrapping a rock in a leaf and gluing him to a piece of bark. Then glue him to the "hay."

- Make a star by using a long piece of reed or raffia. Bend into a star shape and glue it together. Hang the star from the end of a rolled-up vine.

- Add berries to decorate the manger.

TIP: Thick wire does not work.

You will need:
twigs or sticks
vines
berries
dried grass (or raffia)
glue gun
rock
leaves
bark
thin wire

AHEAD OF TIME:
Cut sticks to about eight inches in length.

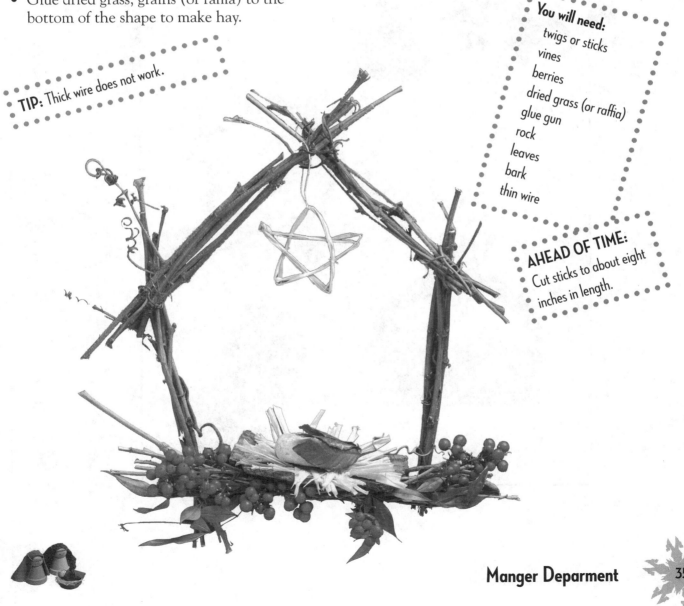

The Christmas Shoppe

Candy Cane Department

Luke 2:8-20

Angels bring good news to the shepherds.

"Nearby shepherds were living in the fields, guarding their sheep at night. The Lord's angel stood before them, the Lord's glory shone around them, and they were terrified."
(Luke 2:8–9)

Directions for Candy Cane Department

The head of the Candy Cane Department will be responsible for organizing the setup of the department prior to the event. The Department Head will also be responsible for the overall supervision of the department during the event.

The Candy Cane Department Head checklist:

❑ Bible storyteller lined up and prepared.

❑ Read The Legend of the Candy Cane and be prepared to tell it.

❑ Candy Cane crafts chosen and all directions and supplies on hand.

❑ Make sure that one sample of each craft is on hand for display.

❑ Supplies laid out by craft (preferably one per table, or end of a long table).

❑ Department Helpers have instructions and know exactly how to do the craft they are helping with. (Or if only one helper, that the helper is familiar with all the crafts.)

❑ Candy Cane patterns photocopied.

❑ Check that children are in the correct department.

> **TIP:** Crafts are listed by abilities rather than ages, because abilities do not necessarily relate directly to age. While guiding younger children to easy-to-manipulate crafts, allow older children some leeway in which candy cane they think they can do well.

DEPARTMENT SESSION OUTLINE

- Children checked as they arrive to ensure they are in the correct department.
- All children sit and storyteller is introduced.
- Storyteller tells story.
- Tell the story of The Legend of the Candy Cane.
- Children directed to appropriate crafts.
- Children make chosen candy canes until time to move to next department or until close of session.

Possible crafts for the Candy Cane Department:

    EASY:
Pompom Candy Cane

    MEDIUM:
Button and Foam Candy Cane

    ADVANCED:
Rolled Paper Candy Cane
Puzzle Piece Candy Cane

Bible Story Script

Welcome! Welcome! I'm the Candy Man (Woman). I'm in charge of all the sugary confections here at The Christmas Shoppe. People just love to come into my shop. They oooh and aaah over the chocolate stars. They stand and drool over the gingerbread houses decorated with icing and gum drops. And their sweet tooth jumps up and down for joy over the caramel crunches. Yes, people love my shop and they love me. You might say that my job is sweet!

But today I'm going to tell you about some people whose job was not sweet. In fact, their job was considered dirty. They spent long hours outside in all kinds of weather. And they were constantly surrounded by smelly animals. Can you guess who I'm talking about? (*Let the children respond.*) That's right. The shepherds.

Well, in today's Bible story the shepherds get a starring role. When Jesus was born in the stable in Bethlehem, there were shepherds watching over their sheep. Remember, I told you shepherds worked long hours. It's because they had to watch the sheep both day and night. During the day they led the sheep to find green grass to eat. Then they led them to find water to drink. They protected the sheep from animals like wolves and lions that wanted to eat the sheep. At night, the shepherds led the sheep into a sheepfold. This was kind of a fenced-in area, or maybe a cave. Anyway one shepherd would lie down in front of the opening to the sheepfold and sleep. That way, none of the sheep could escape in the night.

So back to what happened when Jesus was born. The shepherds were probably lying down for the night when suddenly they saw a bright light. They were afraid! They covered their eyes with their hands and started shaking.

"Don't be afraid," said a voice from the light. "I have good news for you."

It was an angel! The angel told the shepherds that God's Son was born. Then the angel told them to get up, hurry to Bethlehem, and see the baby.

Many, many angels crowded together in the sky. They were singing and praising God. "Glory to God," they sang. "Peace on earth."

The shepherds ran all the way into town. They found Mary and Joseph and baby Jesus. The shepherds worshiped Jesus. Then they told Mary what the angel had said to them. After a while they went back to their sheep, but on the way to the hillside they told everyone they met that God's Son was born.

The Christmas Shoppe

The Legend of the Candy Cane

To many people the candy cane is just colorful candy, but for Christians the candy cane is a symbol of the shepherd's crook. The shepherds were the first to hear the good news that the Savior had been born.

The first candy canes weren't really canes, but straight sticks of sugar candy. How did the cane come to look like a shepherd's crook? Well, in 1670 the choirmaster (we would call him a choir director) in Cologne, Germany, began handing out sugar sticks bent into a shepherd's crook to the children in his choir.

It is said that he gave them these treats to keep the children quiet during church services or as rewards for good behavior. However, the candy canes the choirmaster gave out were plain white.

Candy canes didn't get their stripes until several centuries later. No one knows why they have stripes, but it makes them a lot more fun.

When you put a candy cane on a Christmas tree or you eat one, think of the joy the shepherds felt at the good news of the birth of Jesus.

Pompom Candy Cane

- Using the smaller pattern on page 47, cut a candy cane out of cardboard.

- Punch a hole in the top curve of the cardboard candy cane

- Apply a generous amount of glue to one side of the cardboard candy cane.

- Carefully place each pompom on the cardboard candy cane.

- Thread a ribbon through the hole you punched earlier.

- Allowing enough space to use the ribbon as a hanger, tie a knot in the ribbon at the top.

Button and Foam Candy Cane

- Use the larger candy cane pattern on page 47 to trace a candy cane shape on a craft-foam sheet with a marker.

- Glue buttons (or flat "gems") to the front of the foam candy cane.

- Allow to dry.

- Repeat on opposite side.

You will need:
candy cane pattern (page 47)
craft-foam sheets (red and white)
marker
buttons or flat gems
scissors

TIP: Due to time constraints, one group of children may decorate one side of the candy cane and a second set of children decorate the other side.

Rolled Paper Candy Cane

- Lay a square piece of white paper flat on a tabletop.

- Using a ruler and a red marker, make a line about 1/8-inch thick down the edge of two sides of the paper. The sides must be adjacent.

- Turn the paper over and begin rolling from one corner (without the lines) toward the other corner (with the lines).

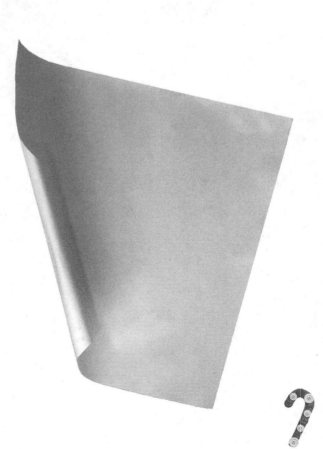

- When completely rolled, tape the corner to keep it in place.

- Wrap one end of the paper tube around a pencil. (Amount to be rolled depends upon size of paper used to make the candy cane.)

- Remove the pencil and adjust the shape to make the curved part of the candy cane. If necessary you may trim off any extra paper at the top and bottom.

Candy Cane Department   45

Puzzle Piece Candy Cane

- Paint seven puzzle pieces white and six puzzle pieces red. (May adapt number according to size of candy cane desired.) Allow to dry.

- Lay out the white pieces first in a candy cane shape.

- Glue red pieces on top of the white pieces. (Generous amounts of glue are recommended.)

- Turn over and add some glue to the back where pieces connect. This will make it sturdier. Allow to dry.

- Cut two pieces of ribbon about eight to ten inches long (depending upon size of candy cane).

- Take one piece of ribbon, fold it in half, and glue the ends to the top back of the candy cane making a hanger for the ornament.

- Use the other piece of ribbon to make a bow for the top of the ornament and glue it to the top front.

- OPTIONAL STEP: Glue a jingle bell to the center of the ribbon.

- Set aside to dry.

You will need:
old jigsaw puzzle pieces
white paint
red paint
paint brush
glue
ribbon
scissors
optional: jingle bells

TIP: Since puzzle pieces must dry, you may wish to spray paint these pieces ahead of time, especially for a one-day event.

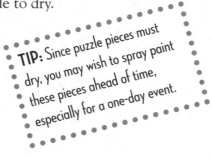

The Christmas Shoppe

Candy Cane Patterns

The Christmas Shoppe

Star Department

Matthew 2:1-12

Wise men come to honor the young child, Jesus.

"We've seen his star in the east, and we've come to honor him." (Matthew 2:2b)

Note: The wise men visited Jesus when he was about two years old. (See Matthew 2:16.) However, having the visit of the wise men celebrated during an Advent or Christmas service is traditional because it completes the story of Jesus' birth. The wise men visiting Jesus are proof indeed that the birth of Jesus was for all humankind.

Directions for Star Department

The head of the Star Department will be responsible for organizing the setup of the department prior to the event. The Department Head will also be responsible for the overall supervision of the department during the event.

The Manger Department Head checklist:

- ❏ Bible storyteller lined up and prepared.
- ❏ Crafts chosen and all directions and supplies on hand.
- ❏ Make sure that one sample of each craft is on hand for display.
- ❏ Supplies laid out by craft (preferably one per table, or end of a long table).
- ❏ Department Helpers have instructions and know exactly how to do the craft they are helping with. (Or if only one helper, that the helper is familiar with all the crafts.)
- ❏ Star patterns photocopied.
- ❏ Check that children are in the correct department.

> **TIP:** Crafts are listed by abilities rather than ages, because abilities do not necessarily relate directly to age. While guiding younger children to easy-to-manipulate crafts, allow older children some leeway in which star they think they can do well.

DEPARTMENT SESSION OUTLINE

- Children checked as they arrive to ensure they are in the correct department.
- All children sit and storyteller is introduced.
- Storyteller tells story.
- Children directed to appropriate crafts.
- Children make chosen stars until time to move to next department or until close of session.

Possible crafts for the Star Department:

EASY:
Straw and Bead Star

MEDIUM:
Corrugated Paper Star
Russian Stick Star

ADVANCED:
3-D Star
Christmas Card Montage Star

Bible Story Script

(Look through a telescope. If you don't have a real telescope, roll a sheet of paper into a tube and make a pretend telescope.)

Star light, star bright, first star I see tonight… Wow! There sure are a lot of stars in the sky. How many do you think there are? millions? billions? trillions? gazillions? I'm not sure, but I know there's a lot.

But wait a minute, I'm getting ahead of myself. I'm Mr. (Mrs.) Polaris. I'm in charge of the Star Department and I just love stars. Have you ever stopped and looked at the stars? Have you found the big dipper and the little dipper? Or maybe Orion's belt? Orion is supposed to be a hunter and his belt is made of three bright stars. Ancient sailors looked at the stars. The north star was an important star for sailors. Knowing where the north star was helped them guide their ships.

Long ago there was another star that was even more important than the north star. There were these astronomers who studied the stars. I don't know how many astronomers there were. The Bible doesn't give us a number, but I think you might know them as the three wise men. Well, as they studied the sky they noticed a star that they had never seen before. It was one star shining brighter than all the other stars. These wise men knew that the star was important. They knew that it meant a king was born.

The wise men got together and decided to find this new king. They wanted to honor him and take him gifts. They chose three gifts—gold, frankincense, and myrrh. I'm sure you know what gold is. Frankincense and myrrh were costly perfumes. Maybe not the best gift for a baby, but good gifts for a king.

The wise men loaded up their camels and began their journey to find the new king. And do you know how they knew which way to go? That's right, they followed that bright star.

The star led them to Jerusalem. The wise men stopped in the city and met with King Herod. "Do you know where the new king is?" they asked.

King Herod was not happy to hear about a new king. He wanted to stay the king himself. But he called together his advisors and asked them about this new king. The advisors told King Herod that the prophets said a new king would be born in Bethlehem. Herod told the wise men to let him know where the new king was living so he could go and worship him, too. Of course, Herod meant to harm the new king, not worship him.

The wise men headed toward Bethlehem. And when they looked up in the sky, there was the star again, guiding them. They followed the star until it stopped over a house in Bethlehem.

They went inside the house and found Mary and Jesus. Jesus was the new king! The wise men gave Jesus their gifts, and then, being warned in a dream about King Herod, they went home a different way.

Straw and Bead Star

- Cut straws into short strips.

- Cut the chenille sticks in half.

- Give each child five precut chenille sticks and the cut pieces of straws and some beads.

- Have the children string the beads and the straw pieces in any combination they like onto the chenille sticks.

- Lay out the five beaded chenille sticks in the shape of a 5-pointed star.

- Twist the ends of the chenille sticks tightly together to hold them in place.

- You may choose to tie a ribbon at the top point of the star to make a tree hanger.

You will need:
colorful plastic drinking straws
chenille sticks
beads
scissors
ribbons

TIP: With younger children, the adult may have to twist the chenille sticks together. Older children can cut the straws themselves.

Corrugated Paper Star

- Trace one large star on one color of corrugated cardboard and one smaller star on a second color of corrugated cardboard.

- Cut out the stars.

- Glue smaller star on top of larger star.

- Punch hole in top of larger star.

> **TIP:** To make stars more interesting, have the waves of the corrugated cardboard stars going in opposite directions.

- Make a simple bow from gold cord. Glue the bow to the center of the top star.

- Glue a button or "gem" on top of the bow.

- Make a small bundle of raffia (see photo below) trimming the ends (staggered lengths are more interesting).

- Tie this small bundle of raffia together with a single piece of raffia.

- Insert the single piece of raffia through the hole in the star and pull it through.

- Tie both ends of the single strand of raffia together to form a loop for hanging the ornament.

> **You will need:**
> corrugated cardboard in two colors
> star patterns - two different sizes (see page 59)
> pencil
> button or "gem"
> raffia
> craft glue
> hole punch
> scissors
> ribbon
> gold cord

> **TIP:** You can use colored markers or crayons to color cardboard if you don't have two different colors.

Russian Stick Star

- Cover the work area with newspaper.

- Cut out a large 5-pointed star using pattern on page 58.

- Color in the star using a mixture of colors with gel markers and/or metallic colored pencils.

- Paint a wooden dowel (gold paint looks good).

- Set star and dowel aside to dry.

- When dry, decorate the star with glitter glue.

- Glue the star to the dowel.

- Cut and glue ribbons to the back of the star to make streamers.

- Allow to dry.

You will need:
newspaper
paper towels
curling ribbon
water
posterboard or old file folders
dowels
paint brushes
metallic colored pencils
gel markers
tempera for dowels
gitter glue
glue

3-D Star

- Cut out two larger stars (exact same size).

- Cut a piece of thread and loop it to make a hanger.

- Place the two large stars back to back, placing the open ends of the thread loop betwen them. Glue the two stars together with the thread ends in the center. (This makes it possible to hang the stars.)

- Cut different size star shapes (in varying papers). How many is up to the individual making the stars.

- Place a pop dot foam adhesive circle in the center of the largest star and stick the second largest star to the center of the first. Place the star at a slightly different position so that the point of the second star comes between the points of the first star.

- Continue stacking stars by size and turning them in this same manner, using the pop dot foam adhesive circles. No special number of stars is required. Let personal taste be your guide.

You will need:
paper scraps in many colors
star patterns in various sizes from pages 58 and 59
pencils
scissors
glue
embroidery floss or metallic thread

OPTIONAL: pop dot adhesives or two-sided tape
(type used for sealing windows)

Christmas Card Montage Star

- Trace the 6-pointed star pattern on the posterboard twice. (Stars must be exact same size.)

- Cut out the two stars.

- Choose designs, words, and figures from the old Christmas cards.

- Cut out the designs, words, and figures and glue them to one of the stars, making a collage. You may wish to place something special in the center of the star.

> **TIP:** Exact fit is not important at this point. Stars will be trimmed later.

- Repeat the process of gluing designs to the second star. On the second star leave the center blank.

- Trim edges of both stars.

- Using the hole punch, punch a hole near the point at the top of the star.

- Glue the completely covered star to the center of the star with the blank center. Stagger the points of the top star to go between the points of the bottom star.

- Outline the edges of the star with glitter paint.

- Thread ribbon through the hole, bring the ends together, and knot to form a hanger for your star ornament.

- Set aside to dry.

Star Patterns

The Christmas Shoppe

Star Patterns

Card Department

Luke 2:15-20

The shepherds tell others about the birth of Jesus.

"Everyone who heard it was amazed at what the shepherds told them." (Luke 2:18)

Note: Children will be hearing the complete story of the shepherds in the Candy Cane Department. In this session the emphasis will be on telling the good news to others.

The Christmas Shoppe

Directions for Card Department

The head of the Card Department will be responsible for organizing the setup of the department prior to the event. The Department Head will also be responsible for the overall supervision of the department during the event.

The Card Department Head checklist:

❑ Bible storyteller lined up and prepared.

❑ Cards to be made chosen and all directions and supplies on hand, including envelopes.

❑ Make sure that one sample of each card is on hand for display.

❑ Supplies laid out by craft (preferably one per table, or end of a long table).

❑ Department Helpers have instructions and know exactly how to make the card they are helping with. (Or if only one helper, that the helper is familiar with all the cards.)

❑ Photocopy pop-up manger pattern on page 72.

❑ Check that children are in the correct department.

TIP: Crafts are listed by abilities rather than ages, because abilities do not necessarily relate directly to age. While guiding younger children to easy-to-manipulate crafts, allow older children some leeway in which card they think they can do well.

DEPARTMENT SESSION OUTLINE

• Children checked as they arrive to ensure they are in the correct department.
• All children sit and storyteller is introduced.
• Storyteller tells story.
• Children directed to appropriate card-making tables.
• Children make chosen cards until time to move to next department or until close of session.

Possible crafts for the Card Department:

EASY:
Hand/Footprint Card
Design Your Angel Card

MEDIUM:
Candy Cane Joy Card
Threaded Stars Card

ADVANCED:
Star Shaped Card
Decorative Words Card
Pop-Up Manger Card
Chenille Stick Baby Jesus

Bible Story Script

Greetings! I'm so glad you stopped by the card department. I'm Hall (Hally) Mark and I'm in charge of this department.

Have you ever had something great happen? Maybe you received a special birthday present. Or maybe you earned an A on a test. What did you do? (*Let the children respond.*) Did you tell a friend all about it. Did you call your grandmother and tell her? That's what I do. When something good happens I want to share it with someone else.

Well, that's just what the shepherds did. Do you remember the shepherds? They were out watching their sheep. Hey, let me hear a few sheep noises. (*Have the children baa.*) And an angel suddenly appeared. Whoa! How do you think the shepherds looked when they saw the angel? (*Encourage the children to show their reactions.*) The angel said, "Don't be afraid. I've got good news!" And the angel told them all about the birth of God's Son. Then the shepherds hurried to Bethlehem (*Encourage the children to run in place or pat their hands on their thighs.*) and found Mary and Joseph and baby Jesus. After the shepherds saw the baby, they praised God. As they went back to their sheep (*Encourage the children to baa.*), they told everyone they met about the angels and baby Jesus.

Do you know what that means? It means a whole lot of people heard about the birth of Jesus. Let me show you what I'm talking about.

(*Choose two children to stand next to you.*) Let's say I tell (*child's name*) and (*child's name*) about the birth of Jesus. How many people know about Jesus' birth? (*3*) Now (*child's name*) and (*child's name*), let's say you each tell two of your friends. (*Let each child pick two friends and have them stand with you.*) Now how many people know about Jesus' birth? (*7*) Now let's say that each of you tell two of your friends. (*Have each child pick two friends and have them stand with you.*) Now how many people know about Jesus' birth? (*15*) (*Keep going with this pattern until all the children are standing with you.*)

And that's how it worked. The angels told the shepherds and the shepherds told their friends and those friends told their friends and so on and so on. And the telling has not stopped in over 2,000 years. We can still tell our family and friends today the good news about Jesus.

Good news! God's Son is born!

The Christmas Shoppe

Hand/Footprint Card

- Have child place both hands on a piece of construction paper and trace around them. Repeat with one bare foot.

- Cut out both hands and the foot. (The hands will become the angel's "wings" and the foot will be the angel's "body.")

- Turn the angel's body over and write a message such as "Merry Christmas" on the back. Then turn it back to the front.

- Glue the hands to the heel of the foot with the fingers out, forming wings.

- Draw a "head" on another sheet of paper. (An adult may have to help the children get the proportion correct.)

- Draw a face on the head.

- Glue the face to the heel of the foot.

- From different colors of construction paper, cut out hair and a halo and glue to the angel's head.

- Cut out a strip of paper. (This forms a name "banner.")

- Write the name of the person making the angel on the banner and decorate it with crayons and glitter glue.

- Glue the name banner across the front of the angel.

You will need:
construction paper
markers or crayons (some multiracial crayons)
glue
glitter glue
scissors

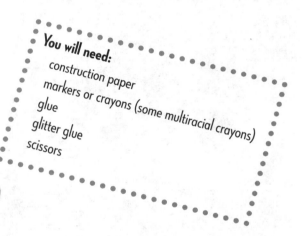

Design Your Angel Card

- Lay out card supplies.

- Challenge children to design their own angel.

- Encourage using a pencil to draw an angel outline. For younger children you may use an angel pattern on page 67.

- Let them decorate their angel in any style they would like.

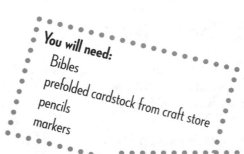

You will need:
Bibles
prefolded cardstock from craft store
pencils
markers

OPTIONAL:
glitter pens
decorative trim
sequins
glitter
ribbon
scissors
angel pattern

OPTIONAL: Have older children use their Bibles to look up the Christmas story and add a Bible verse of their choosing to their card.

Angel Patterns

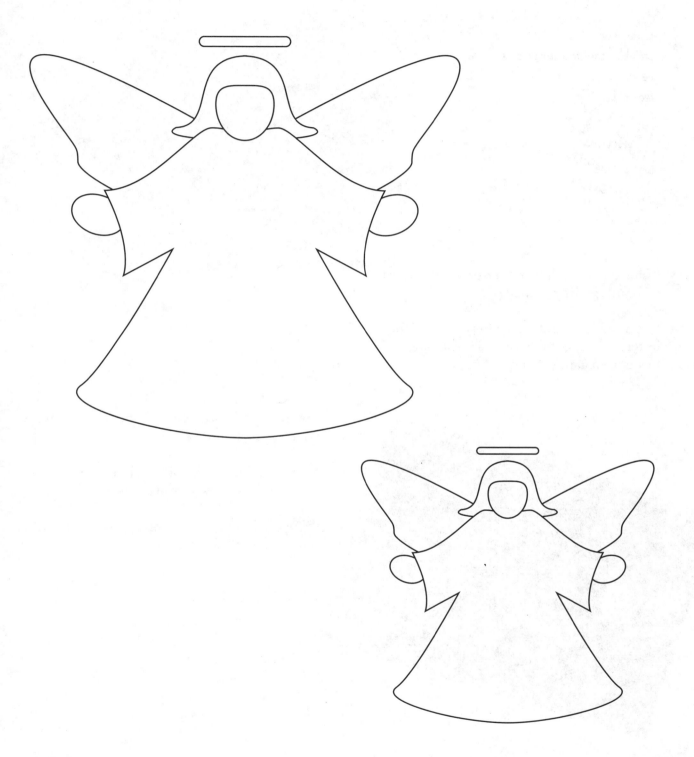

Card Department

Candy Cane Joy Card

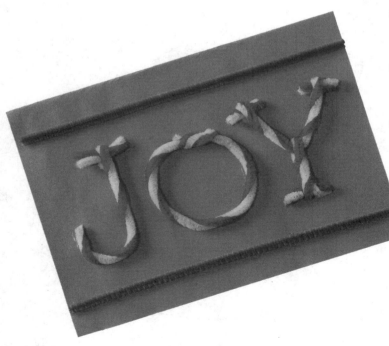

- Using a pencil, draw fat letters on the front of the card spelling JOY.

- Use a red marker to color in stripes on the letters, making them look as if they were made from candy canes.

OPTION:

- Twist together one red and one white chenille stick for each letter in the word JOY.

- Shape each set of chenille sticks into one of the letters. Use scissors to trim as needed.

- Glue the letters to the front of the card and set aside to dry.

Threaded Stars Card

- Using a pencil draw a small star using a pattern from page 59.

- Cut out three stars from colored paper (construction paper or art paper will work best)

- Punch a hole in two of the points on each star (see design below).

- Cut glittery thread or tinsel long enough to thread through all the holes. It will look like your stars are hanging in a row from a glittery rope.

- Glue the ends of the thread or tinsel to the backs of the end stars.

- Glue threaded stars in a row to the front of the card.

- Below the stars use a fine-tip marker to write, "We have seen his star."

You will need:
prefolded cardstock from craft store
colored paper
pencils
star patterns (page 59)
hole punch
glittery thread or thin tinsel
scissors
glue
fine-tip markers

Star Shaped Card

- Using the star patterns, cut out: three large stars, one star on design cardstock, one on solid-color cardstock, and one on white card stock.

- Using a medium star pattern, cut one medium star on design cardstock.

- Cut a 4-inch long pice of ribbon and fold it in half. Glue one end of the ribbon near the top of one side of the large white star.

You will need:
2 types of design cardstock (different patterns, holographic, striped, and so forth.)
solid-colored cardstock
white cardstock
¼-inch wide ribbon
10 gold mini brads
scissors
pencil
glue gun
star pattern (see page 59)
double-sided tape

- Glue the other end of the ribbon near the top of the same side of the white star.

- Glue the design cardstock and white cardstock stars together covering and hiding the ribbon. The white side is the back of the card.

- Place a gold brad on each tip of the large solid-color star. Repeat with the design star.

- Place double-sided tape (or glue) on back of large solid-color star. (Place the star so that the star tips of each star alternate.)

- Repeat with medium-sized star on top of large solid-color star. Use double-sided tape (or glue) to fasten the medium star so that the large solid-color star looks as if it is the border of the medium star.

Decorative Words Card

Encourage children to use their imaginations to create Christmas cards consisting totally of words.

Some possible words: JOY, HOPE, LOVE, PEACE, JESUS, PRINCE OF PEACE, PEACE ON EARTH, SAVIOR

Lay out all craft materials and let each child decide how he or she will create a card. Here are some possible methods:

- Use colored markers or glitter pens to write one word (or many words) on the front of the card.

- Write a word with a pencil on the front of the card, making the letters fat and open so they may be filled in. Outline each letter with black markers. Cut or tear scraps of Christmas wrapping paper and fill in the letters.

- Write a word (again making large open letters) and outline with decorative trim. Glitter may be applied to the inside of these letters.

- Any combination of the above, or allow children to create their own ideas.

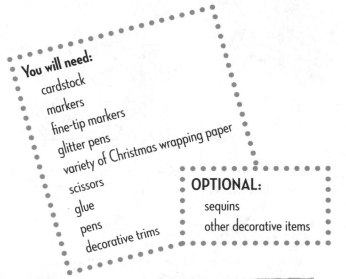

You will need:
- cardstock
- markers
- fine-tip markers
- glitter pens
- variety of Christmas wrapping paper
- scissors
- glue
- pens
- decorative trims

OPTIONAL:
- sequins
- other decorative items

Pop-Up Manger Card

- Fold the smaller piece of construction paper in half crosswise. Fold each end to the center.

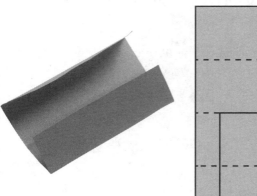 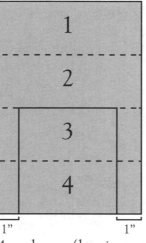

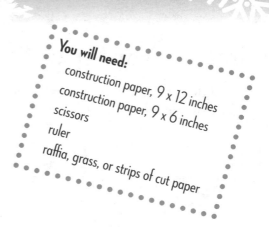

- Glue raffia, grass, or small cut-up strips of paper in the manger to form "hay."

- Make a chenille stick baby Jesus to go in the manger. (See page 73.)

- Cut out sections 3 and 4 as shown (leaving only a 1-inch strip on each side).

- Fold the 1-inch sections in a triangle, so that they overlap section 4. Paste them in place forming a manger. (See the illustration.)

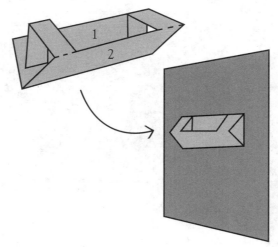

- Paste section 1 of the folded and cut paper above the center on the large piece of construction paper. The manger will be on the inside top half of the card.

Chenille Stick Baby Jesus

For each baby Jesus you will need:
2 chenille stems

OPTIONAL:
small piece of cloth
(or a Kleenex)

- Make a loop in the center of the first chenille stick. This will be the head and arms of baby Jesus.

- Thread the second chenille stick through the loop and bend double.

- Twist the second chenille stick two to four turns. This forms the body. Leave a portion of this chenille stick below the body for the legs.

- You may glue the "baby" directly in the manger as is or wrap tightly in a small piece of cloth and glue it into the manger.

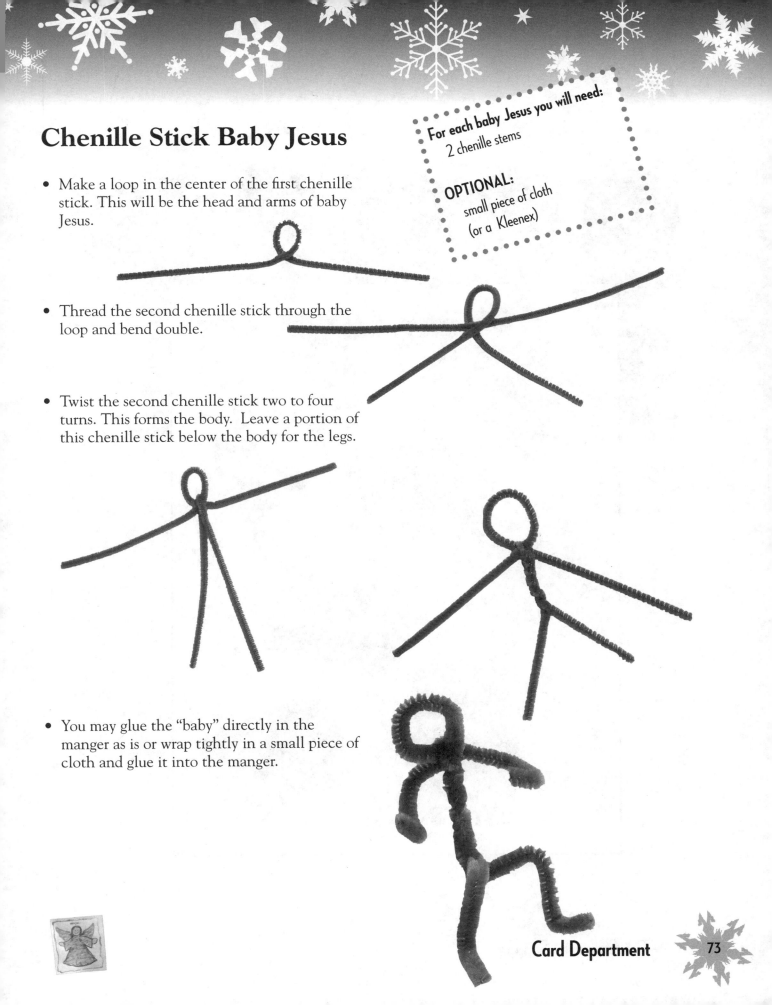

The Christmas Shoppe

Bakery Department

Isaiah 9:2-6

Prophets proclaim the birth of the Messiah.

"A child is born to us, a son is given to us, and authority will be on his shoulders. He will be named Wonderful Counselor, Mighty God, Eternal Father, Prince of Peace." (Isaiah 9:6)

Directions for Bakery Department

The Head Baker will be responsible for organizing the setup of the department prior to the event. The Head Baker will also be responsible for the overall supervision of the department during the event.

Head Baker Checklist:

❑ Bible storyteller lined up and prepared.

❑ Ingredients purchased and necessary utensils on hand.

❑ Department Helpers have instructions and know exactly how to make each item.

❑ Photocopy patterns for the angel jar tags on page 80, the hot chocolate recipe on page 82, and for the manger cookies on page 84.

❑ Check that children are in the correct department.

TIP: Crafts are listed by abilities rather than ages, because abilities do not necessarily relate directly to age. While guiding younger children to easy-to-manipulate crafts, allow older children some leeway in which craft they think they can do well.

DEPARTMENT SESSION OUTLINE

- Children checked as they arrive to ensure they are in the correct department.
- All children sit and storyteller is introduced.
- Storyteller tells story.
- Children directed to appropriate tables.
- Children work on items until time to move to next department or until close of session.

TIP: Because of time factors some items may have to be started by one group and finished by another.

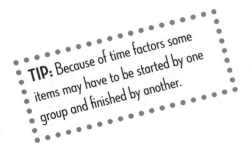

Possible crafts for the Bakery Department:

EASY:
Flavored Popcorn with Decorative Jar

MEDIUM:
Hot Chocolate Mix With Candy Cane Stirrers
Chocolate Candy Cane Sticks
Chocolate Manger Cookies

ADVANCED:
Star Melts

Bible Story Script

Hello, boys and girls. Welcome to the bakery. I'm the Head Baker here at The Christmas Shoppe, Mrs. (Mr.) Quick. Even though my name is Quick, it doesn't pay to be in a hurry when I'm baking. Baking bread, cookies, cakes, and pies takes a lot of patience and "wait time." You have to wait almost an hour for the bread to rise before you can bake it. Then you have to wait another thirty minutes for the bread to bake. But the wait is worth it. I love the smell of fresh-baked bread, and I especially love the way it tastes.

Would you like to try some? (*Hand out pieces of bread to the children.*) What do you think? Was it worth the wait?

The people in Bible times knew about "wait time." Especially the prophets. Do you know what a prophet is? A prophet is someone who speaks for God. The prophet Isaiah told the people that God promised to send a messiah, a new kind of king, to lead them.

Isaiah said, "The people walking in darkness have seen a great light." Have you ever tried walking in the dark? It's kind of scary isn't it? But what if you have a flashlight? Turning on the flashlight allows you to see where you're going.

With the light, walking in the dark is not so scary. Isaiah was saying that God promised to send a leader who would help the people not be afraid.

Then Isaiah said something surprising. He said that this new kind of king would be a child! "A child is born to us; a son is given to us, and authority will be on his shoulders. He will be named Wonderful Counselor, Mighty God, Eternal Father, Prince of Peace" (Isaiah 9:6).

The people wanted this new leader to come right away, but they had to wait. They waited and they waited. Finally, after several hundred years the child Isaiah told the people about was born. Do you know who that child was? That's right. The child was Jesus. Do you think Jesus was worth the wait? Definitely!

A child is born to us—and that child was Jesus. And today we don't have to wait to celebrate Jesus.

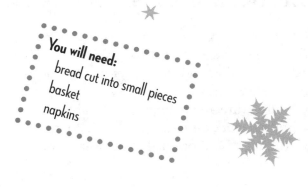

You will need:
bread cut into small pieces
basket
napkins

Flavored Popcorn With Decorative Jar

Amount of popcorn and ingredients are subjective. How much popcorn do you need to make and how thick do you want the coating?

CHEESY POPCORN
- Pour Parmesan cheese over plain popcorn.

SWEET GLAZED POPCORN
- Melt butter and brown sugar.
- Drizzle over popcorn and stir.

CHOCOLATE POPCORN
- Make sweet glaze above and add some chocolate drink mix.
- Drizzle over popcorn and stir.
- Grate white and dark chocolate over the glazed popcorn.

You will need:
popcorn
popcorn popper or microwave
mixing bowls
cookie sheets
spoons and/or spatulas

TIP: For flavored popcorn begin by spreading the popped corn on a cookie sheet and place in a warm oven while making the topping. Topping sticks better to hot popcorn.

For Cheesy Popcorn:
Parmesan cheese

Sweet Glazed Popcorn:
butter
brown sugar

Chocolate Corn:
butter
brown sugar
chocolate drink mix
white and dark chocolate

Angel Jar

- Wash and dry jars and lids thoroughly.

- Decorate the jars with stickers.

- Place flavored popcorn in jars and put lids on tightly.

- Color the angel on the tag and write the flavor of popcorn in the jar on the tag.

- Punch hole in tag and thread through with colored ribbon.

- Tie the ribbon with the angel tag around the jar (probably best to tie it close to the lid). You may wish to tape the ribbon onto the jar in one spot to secure it.

OPTION: Use inexpensive decorative tins and wrap the ribbon with the tag around the middle of the tin. Secure with tape.

You will need:
glass or plastic jars with lids
stickers
angel tags (page 80)
scissors
colored markers
hole punch
ribbon

Angel Jar Tags

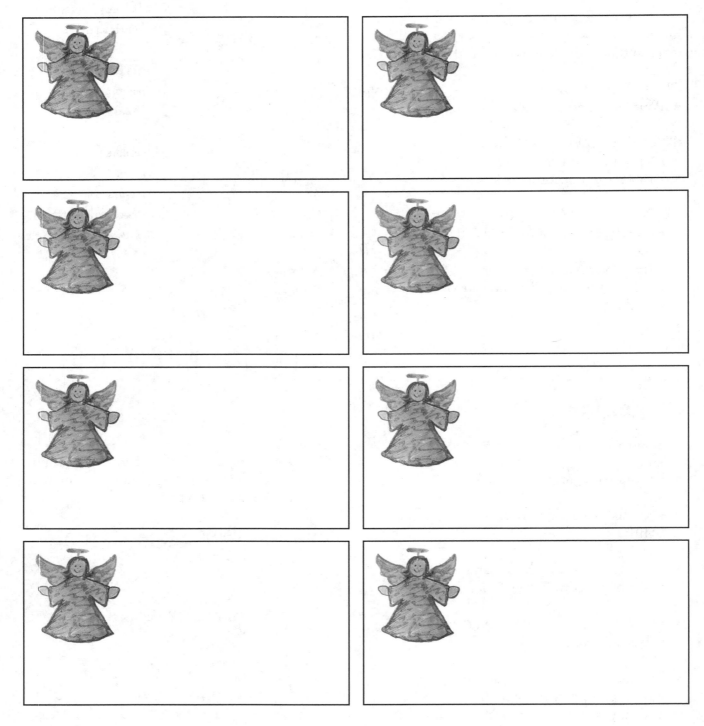

Hot Chocolate Mix With Candy Cane Stirrers

Ingredients:

(for approximately 45 servings)

10 cups powered milk

4 ¾ cups sifted
  confectioner's sugar

1 ¾ cups non-dairy creamer (powdered)

1 ¾ cups powdered cocoa

- Combine milk powder, confectioner's sugar, creamer, and cocoa.

- Stir thoroughly.

- Divide into about ten servings (⅓ cup per serving) per plastic sandwich bag.

- Place a hot chocolate tag (from page 82) and one or two candy canes for stirrers inside each bag before sealing the bag.

You will need:

a large bowl

stirrers

plastic sandwich bags

hot chocolate tags (page 82)

candy canes

OPTIONAL:

pretied bows

tape (to fasten bows to bags)

paper bags

OPTIONAL: Place a plastic bag with the mix and two candy canes into a colorful small paper bag (such as found in dollar stores). Tape the tag to the paper bag.

TIP: You may wish to add a small pretied bow to each bag.

Hot Chocolate Tags

For 1 serving of hot chocolate use
⅓ cup cocoa mix and ¾ cup boiling water
per cup.

This bag contains _____ servings.

For 1 serving of hot chocolate use
⅓ cup cocoa mix and ¾ cup boiling water
per cup.

This bag contains _____ servings.

For 1 serving of hot chocolate use
⅓ cup cocoa mix and ¾ cup boiling water
per cup.

This bag contains _____ servings.

For 1 serving of hot chocolate use
⅓ cup cocoa mix and ¾ cup boiling water
per cup.

This bag contains _____ servings.

For 1 serving of hot chocolate use
⅓ cup cocoa mix and ¾ cup boiling water
per cup.

This bag contains _____ servings.

For 1 serving of hot chocolate use
⅓ cup cocoa mix and ¾ cup boiling water
per cup.

This bag contains _____ servings.

For 1 serving of hot chocolate use
⅓ cup cocoa mix and ¾ cup boiling water
per cup.

This bag contains _____ servings.

For 1 serving of hot chocolate use
⅓ cup cocoa mix and ¾ cup boiling water
per cup.

This bag contains _____ servings.

The Christmas Shoppe

Chocolate Candy Cane Sticks

This recipe makes about fifteen candy cane sticks.

- Place 1 cup of chocolate chips and 1 teaspoon of vegetable oil in a bowl.

- Microwave for one minute, stir, then microwave for ten seconds. Repeat until most (but not all) of the chocolate chips have melted.

- Stir until the chocolate is smooth.

- Spread sprinkles (nonpareils) on a sheet of wax paper.

- Dip the end of the unwrapped candy cane into the chocolate, them roll into the sprinkles.

- Place on a clean sheet of wax paper and allow to dry.

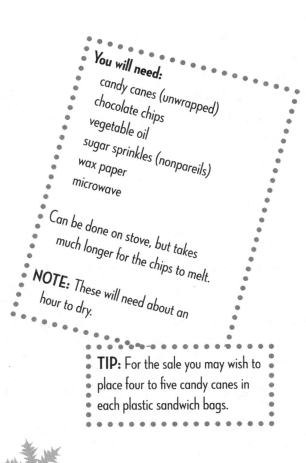

You will need:
candy canes (unwrapped)
chocolate chips
vegetable oil
sugar sprinkles (nonpareils)
wax paper
microwave

Can be done on stove, but takes much longer for the chips to melt.

NOTE: These will need about an hour to dry.

TIP: For the sale you may wish to place four to five candy canes in each plastic sandwich bags.

Star Melts

You will need:
- peppermint candies
- oven (small toaster oven works well)
- baking sheet
- aluminum foil
- metal star-shaped cookie cutters
- spray cooking oil
- plastic sandwich bags

TIP: Cookie cutters must be metal.

- Preheat oven to 325 degrees.

- Cover baking sheet with aluminum foil.

- Coat metal star-shaped cookie cutters with spray cooking oil.

- Place several peppermint candies inside the cookie cutters on the aluminum foil covered baking sheets.

- Bake 6–7 minutes.

- Allow cookies to cool. When cool, pop out the Star Melts.

- Place inside of plastic sandwich bags for the sale.

OPTION: You may wish to make Angel Melts or other shapes, depending upon available cookie cutters.

The Christmas Shoppe

Chocolate Manger Cookies

Ingredients (per batch):

2½ cups flour

⅓ cup cocoa powder (unsweetend)

½ teaspoon salt

1 cup sugar

2 sticks of butter, softened

1 large egg

1 teaspoon vanilla

- Beat butter and sugar until pale and fluffy. (Easiest to do with a mixer, but older children may take turns beating it with a spatula.)

- In a large bowl stir together the flour, cocoa powder, and salt.

- Add the egg and vanilla to the butter and sugar mixture and mix. (This step is easily done with a spatula by any age child.)

- Add the flour mixture to the butter and sugar mixture.

- Mix together thoroughly.

- Shape the dough into two balls; wrap each ball in plastic wrap.

- Refrigerate for at least one hour.

NOTE: You will have to make the dough in time to chill it the first time unless you are having an all-day event and different groups will be working on different parts of the process. If you make ahead it will keep well in the refrigerator overnight.

To make manger:

- Cut out the cookie patterns.

- Roll out cookie dough and lay patterns on top. (Dough should be about ¼ of an inch thick.)

- Using a knife, cut out the rectangle and roof to make a "manger." (You might wish to chill for another 30 minutes.)

- Bake on greased baking sheet at 350 degrees for about ten minutes (or until cookies are firm). DO NOT OVERBAKE.

OPTIONAL: Press a small yellow candy into the "roof" right under the point to represent a star. You may also wish to make a "door outline" by using a toothpick and white icing. Or you may use the toothpick to outline a door and spread yellow icing inside this door to indicate light coming from the inside.

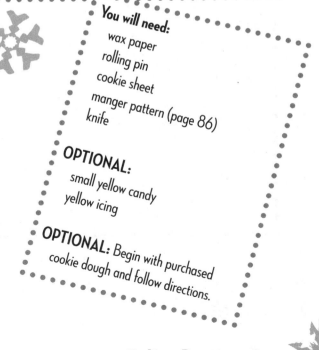

You will need:

wax paper

rolling pin

cookie sheet

manger pattern (page 86)

knife

OPTIONAL:

small yellow candy

yellow icing

OPTIONAL: Begin with purchased cookie dough and follow directions.

Manger Cookie Patterns

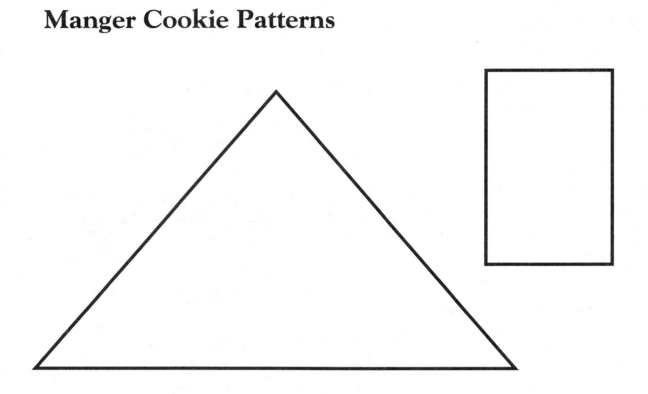

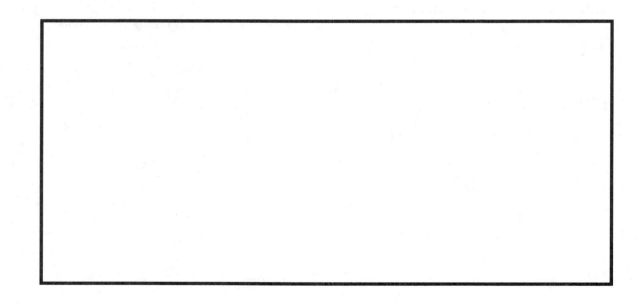

The Christmas Shoppe

Forms
and Other
Useful
Information

Department Assignment Cards

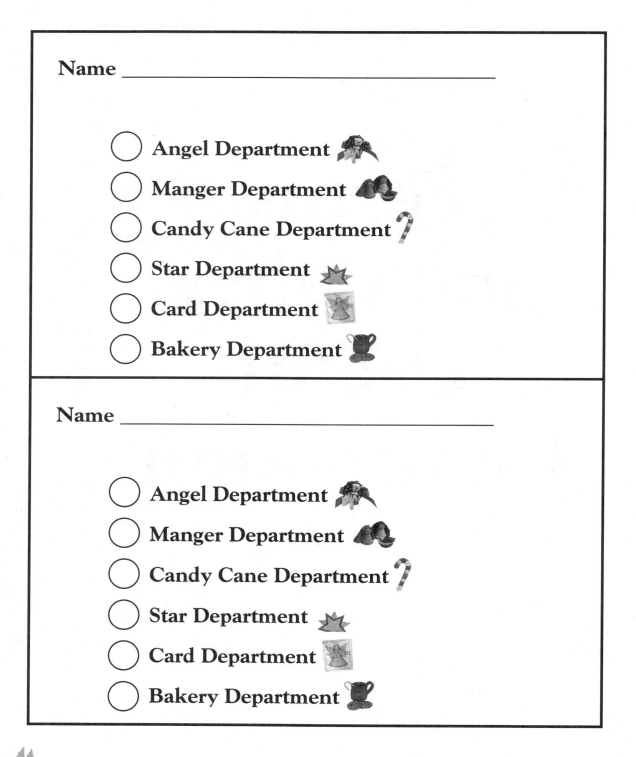

Name _____

○ **Angel Department**

○ **Manger Department**

○ **Candy Cane Department**

○ **Star Department**

○ **Card Department**

○ **Bakery Department**

Name _____

○ **Angel Department**

○ **Manger Department**

○ **Candy Cane Department**

○ **Star Department**

○ **Card Department**

○ **Bakery Department**

Christmas Shoppe Department Rotation Tips

- Children may be rotated through the departments by age or by mixed ages. This will depend upon the number of participants and the number of helpers in each department.

- So that children and leaders alike can track if children are in the correct department use, the Department Assignment Form on page 88.

- Photocopy and cut apart the forms. You will need one form per child.

- Before registration, place a number in the circle in front of the departments. This will tell the children and the Department Heads in what order they are to visit each department.

- Ask Department Heads to check each form as children enter their department.

- If you are doing fewer departments than listed on the form, use the form as a model to make your own.

- Have only a small number of children? You may wish to rotate them as a group or only two groups through the departments in succession.

Registration Form

CHILD'S NAME _____

PARENT/GUARDIAN NAME _____

CONTACT PHONE NUMBER _____

ALTERNATIVE _____

ALLERGIES OR OTHER IMPORTANT MEDICAL
INFORMATION: _____

_____

Parent/Guardian Signature

Registration Form

CHILD'S NAME _____

PARENT/GUARDIAN NAME _____

CONTACT PHONE NUMBER _____

ALTERNATIVE _____

ALLERGIES OR OTHER IMPORTANT MEDICAL
INFORMATION: _____

_____

Parent/Guardian Signature

The Children of

_____

invite you to our
Grand Christmas Shoppe Sale

Where: _____

Day: _____

Hours of Operation: _____

In honor of the birth of Jesus, our Savior,
all proceeds will go to

_____

Mission Project Checklist

Check with mission committee and/or church staff regarding how project fits into your church's overall Christmas mission.

Assigned to: _____

Check with the chosen organization regarding needs and information on donating money or gifts. (This may be available through church office if working with existing mission.)

Assigned to: _____

Getting the Word Out:

Who to: (parents only, whole congregation, surrounding community)

How:

Newsletter assigned to: _____

E-mail blasts assigned to: _____

Posters assigned to: _____

Other: _____

_____

The Christmas Shoppe Master Crafts Supply List

- ❏ Advent wreath
- ❏ bark
- ❏ beads (in at least two sizes)
- ❏ beads (pony and flat)
- ❏ berries (from craft store)
- ❏ Bibles
- ❏ boxes
- ❏ brads (gold, mini)
- ❏ butane lighter
- ❏ buttons or flat gems
- ❏ candles (4 purple or blue)
- ❏ candle snuffer
- ❏ cardboard or recycled cereal boxes
- ❏ chenille stems/sticks
- ❏ Christmas cards (used)
- ❏ coffee filters
- ❏ cord (gold)
- ❏ cotton balls, jumbo
- ❏ corrugated cardboard in two colors
- ❏ crayons (multiracial)
- ❏ curling ribbon (red, white, brown, black, yellow, gold)
- ❏ disks
- ❏ doilies (four-inch)
- ❏ drinking straws
- ❏ dowels
- ❏ fabric scraps (some light colored)
- ❏ embroidery floss or metallic thread
- ❏ foam sheets (from craft store)
- ❏ gel markers
- ❏ glitter pens
- ❏ glittery thread or thin tinsel

- ❏ glue (glitter, white, and tacky)
- ❏ glue gun and glue for gun
- ❏ hole punch
- ❏ jigsaw puzzle (used)
- ❏ knobs (wooden, two sizes for Nativity figures)
- ❏ leaves
- ❏ lollipops (chocolate-filled, fruit-flavored)
- ❏ markers (all types: including fine-tip, permanent; red)
- ❏ paint:
    red and white, glitter, and tempera
- ❏ paint brushes
- ❏ paint pens
- ❏ paper:
    Christmas wrapping
    construction
    cardstock (two different designs)
    cardstock (prefolded)
    scraps in many colors)
    newspaper
    white (8½ by 11 inches)
- ❏ paper clip clamps
- ❏ paper towels
- ❏ pencils
    sharpened
    unsharpened (new)
    metallic colored
- ❏ pens
    - ❏ pompoms (1 inch, red and white)
- ❏ posterboard (or file folders)

- ❏ pots (small terra cotta or plastic for nativity)
- ❏ quilting thread or jewelry wire
- ❏ raffia (or dried grass)
- ❏ ribbon
    1-inch
    various sizes and colors for ornament hangers
    ¼ inch wire-edged
- ❏ rings (gold-colored metal)
- ❏ rocks
- ❏ rulers
- ❏ safety pins
- ❏ saucers (small terra cotta or plastic for Nativity)
- ❏ scissors
- ❏ sequins (for eyes)
- ❏ sticks or twigs
- ❏ stapler and staples
- ❏ tape (clear and double-sided)
- ❏ thin wire
- ❏ tinsel stems
- ❏ vines
- ❏ water
- ❏ yarn
    thinner "skin" colored
    bulky weight yarn
    red
- OPTIONAL:
- ❏ decorative trim
- ❏ fabric roses (small)
- ❏ glitter
- ❏ jingle bells
- ❏ metallic thread
- ❏ pop dot adhesives

The Christmas Shoppe Master Supply List
Bakery Items and Patterns

Bakery Items

Food Items
- ❑ bread cut into small pieces
- ❑ butter
- ❑ candy (hard, yellow, for star)
- ❑ candy canes
- ❑ chocolate
  - dark
  - white
- ❑ chocolate chips
- ❑ chocolate drink mix
- ❑ cocoa (powdered, unsweetened)
- ❑ cooking oil spray
- ❑ creamer, non diary (powdered)
- ❑ eggs, large
- ❑ flour (all purpose, for cookies)
- ❑ icing (white, yellow food coloring)
- ❑ Parmesan cheese
- ❑ peppermint candies
- ❑ powdered milk
- ❑ salt
- ❑ sugar
  - white granular
  - brown
  - confectioner's
- ❑ sprinkles
- ❑ unpopped popcorn
- ❑ vanilla
- ❑ vegetable oil

OPTIONAL:
- ❑ Purchased cookie dough for manger cookies

Non-Food Items
- ❑ aluminum foil
- ❑ baking sheet
- ❑ basket
- ❑ colored markers
- ❑ cookie cutters, metal, star-shaped
- ❑ cookie sheets
- ❑ glass jars with lids
- ❑ hole punch
- ❑ hot chocolate tags
- ❑ knife (table knife will work)
- ❑ mixing bowls
- ❑ napkins
- ❑ oven
- ❑ patterns to reproduce:
- ❑ plastic bags
- ❑ plastic sandwich bags
- ❑ popcorn popper or microwave
- ❑ ribbon
- ❑ rolling pins
- ❑ spoons and spatulas
- ❑ stickers
- ❑ stirrers
- ❑ wax paper or butter (for cookies sheets)
- ❑ angel tags

OPTIONAL:
- ❑ pretied bows
- ❑ tape
- ❑ stone box manger

Angel Department Supply List

- ❑ beads (in two sizes)
- ❑ beads (pony and flat)
- ❑ cardboard (cut in six-by-two-inch pieces)
- ❑ chenille stems
- ❑ coffee filters
- ❑ construction paper
- ❑ cord (gold)
- ❑ curling ribbon (red, white, brown, black, yellow, or gold)
- ❑ disks
- ❑ doilies (four-inch)
- ❑ fabric (light-colored)
- ❑ glue (white)
- ❑ lollipops (chocolate-filled, fruit-flavored)
- ❑ markers (fine-tip felt)
- ❑ paper clip clamps
- ❑ pencils (unsharpened, new)
- ❑ quilting thread or jewelry wire
- ❑ ribbon
    - 1-inch ribbon for bows
    - ¼-inch wire-edged ribbon for angel wings
    - ribbon, various sizes and colors
- ❑ safety pins
- ❑ stapler and staples
- ❑ scissors
- ❑ tinsel stems
- ❑ yarn

OPTIONAL:
- ❑ fabric roses (small)

Manger Department Supply List

- bark
- berries (from craft store)
- chenille sticks
- construction paper (yellow)
- cotton balls, jumbo
- embroidery floss
- fabric scraps
- glue (white)
- glue (tacky)
- glue gun and glue for gun
- hole punch
- knobs (wooden, two sizes for Nativity figures)
- leaves
- markers, brown, gray, black (washable and permanent)
- paint pens
- pots (small: terra cotta or plastic for Nativity)
- raffia (or dried grass)
- rocks
- rulers
- saucer (small: terra cotta or plastic for Nativity)
- scissors
- sequins (for eyes)
- sticks or twigs
- thin wire
- vines
- white paper
- yarn (finer "skin" colored yarn, bulky yarn)
- box manger pattern

Candy Cane Department Supply List

- buttons or flat gems
- candy cane patterns
- cardboard or recycled cereal boxes
- foam sheets (from craft store)
- tacky glue
- hole punch
- jigsaw puzzle pieces (used)
- markers (some red)
- paint (red and white)
- paint brushes
- pencils
- pompoms (1-inch, red and white)
- ribbon
- rulers
- scissors
- tape
- white paper

OPTIONAL:
- jingle bells
- red yarn

Star Department Supply List

- beads
- buttons or "gems"
- chenille sticks
- Christmas cards (used)
- cord (gold)
- corrugated cardboard (two different colors)
  or cardboard and crayons
- dowels (wooden)
- drinking straws
- embroidery floss or metallic thread
- gel markers
- glitter paint
- glue
- hole punch
- newspaper
- paint brushes
- paper scraps in many colors
- paper towels
- pencils
  regular
  metallic colored
- posterboard (or old file folders)
- raffia
- ribbons
- scissors
- star patterns of all sizes
- tempera
- water

OPTIONAL:
- pop dot adhesives or two-sided tape (type used for sealing windows)

Card Department Supply List

- ❑ angel pattern
- ❑ Bibles
- ❑ brads (gold, mini)
- ❑ cardstock (prefolded, white, 2 designs)
- ❑ Christmas wrapping paper (wide variety of colors and designs)
- ❑ chenille stems (red and white)
- ❑ construction paper
- ❑ double-sided tape
- ❑ glitter glue
- ❑ glitter pens
- ❑ glittery thread or thin tinsel
- ❑ glue
- ❑ glue gun
- ❑ markers or crayons (regular and fine-tip, some multiracial, some red)
- ❑ pencils
- ❑ pens
- ❑ raffia (grass, or strips of cut paper)
- ❑ ribbon, ¼-inch
- ❑ rings (large, gold-colored)
- ❑ rulers
- ❑ scissors

OPTIONAL:
- ❑ chenille stems for baby Jesus
- ❑ cloth (small scraps or tissue)
- ❑ decorative trims
- ❑ glitter
- ❑ ribbon
- ❑ sequins

Note: For Pop-up Manger Cards you will need some 9 x 12-inch construction paper.

Bakery Department Bakery Items Supply List

Food Items

- bread cut into small pieces
- butter
- candy (hard, yellow, for star on cookie manger)
- candy canes
- chocolate (dark/white)
- chocolate chips
- chocolate drink mix
- cocoa (powdered, unsweetened)
- cooking oil, spray
- creamer, nondiary (powdered)
- eggs, large
- flour (all purpose, for cookies)
- icing (white, yellow food coloring)
- Parmesan cheese
- peppermint candies
- powdered milk
- salt
- sugar
  white granular
  brown
  confectioner's
- sprinkles
- unpopped popcorn
- vanilla
- vegetable oil

OPTIONAL:
- purchased cookie dough for manger cookies

Non Food Items

- aluminum foil
- angel tags
- basket
- colored markers
- cookie cutters, metal, star-shaped
- cookie sheets
- glass jars with lids
- hole punch
- hot chocolate tags
- knife (table knife will work)
- mixing bowls
- napkins
- oven
- plastic bags
- plastic sandwich bags
- popcorn popper or microwave
- scissors
- spoons and spatulas
- stickers
- stirrers
- ribbon
- wax paper or butter (for cookies sheets)
- manger cookie patterns

OPTIONAL:
- pretied bows
- tape

The Grand Christmas Shoppe Sale Setup List

❑ tables for each department

❑ tablecloths for each department table

❑ signs for each department table

❑ price tags for items (Colored dots like those used at garage sales make pricing easier. Just post a sign with the price of each color.)

❑ box of change for each department table (or set up a designated check-out table and have one box of change)

❑ plastic bags for items sold

❑ tissue paper for wrapping any fragile items

❑ Make assignments for someone to supervise at each table and/or someone to collect money at the check-out table.

Note: You will make a lot more money at your sale if you label a basket that says "donations" and don't bother to price items.

Use of CD-ROM With Worship

The CD-ROM contains the worship scripts.
The scripts are also on pages 103 through 109 of
this book. They are provided both ways for your
convenience.

The script is the same for each department, but
the section a department is responsible for is
highlighted in that department's script.

NOTE: Page 103 contains an outline
of the worship service for the use of the
director and those helping with lighting,
PowerPoint®, and so forth

For your convenience, the CD-ROM contains
a PowerPoint® that contains the music and the
words for the songs to be used in the closing
worship.

You may use this music without practice, as the
songs are easy for children and adults alike.

If you wish, you may substitute your own music
for worship.

Worship Presentation Outline

Greeting

Explanation of the chosen mission project and purpose of the sale

Lighting of Advent wreath candles with reading (See page 14.)

Congregational Singing: "Let's Get Ready, A Savior's Coming"

Scripture: Matthew 1:18-24 and Luke 1:26-38

Congregational Singing: "Angel Band"

> Angel Department brings angel ornaments forward.

Scripture: Luke 2:1-7

Congregational Singing: "Away in a Manger"

> Manger Department brings manger ornaments forward.

Reading of The Legend of the Candy Cane. (See page 41.)

Scripture: Luke 2:8-20

Congregational Singing: "Bethlehem"

> Candy Cane Department brings candy cane ornaments forward.

Scripture: Matthew 2:1-12

Congregational Singing: "We Three Kings"

> Star Department brings star ornaments forward.

Scripture: Luke 2:15-20

Congregational Singing: "Go, Tell It on the Mountain"

> Card Department brings cards forward.

Congregational Singing: "Joy to the World"

> Bakery Department brings baked goods forward.

Benediction: Isaiah 9:2-6

TIPS: Assign an older child from each department to read the Scripture associated with that department. The Legend of the Candy Cane should be read by a child. Because of the sale, you may wish to have just one of each kind of ornament brought forward as a representation of what has been done. Have these placed on trays on the altar for easy transfer to the sale area.

Worship Presentation Outline
ANGEL DEPARTMENT

Greeting

Explanation of the chosen mission project and purpose of the sale

Lighting of Advent wreath candles with reading

Congregational Singing: "Let's Get Ready, A Savior's Coming"

Scripture: Matthew 1:18-24 and Luke 1:26-38

Congregational Singing: "Angel Band"

Angel Department brings angel ornaments forward.

Scripture: Luke 2:1-7

Congregational Singing: "Away in a Manger"

Manger Department brings manger ornaments forward.

Reading of The Legend of the Candy Cane.

Scripture: Luke 2:8-20

Congregational Singing: "Bethlehem"

Candy Cane Department brings candy cane ornaments forward.

Scripture: Matthew 2:1-12

Congregational Singing: "We Three Kings"

Star Department brings star ornaments forward.

Scripture: Luke 2:15-20

Congregational Singing: "Go, Tell It on the Mountain"

Card Department brings cards forward.

Congregational Singing: "Joy to the World"

Bakery Department brings baked goods forward.

Benediction: Isaiah 9:2-6

Worship Presentation Outline
MANGER DEPARTMENT

Greeting

Explanation of the chosen mission project and purpose of the sale

Lighting of Advent wreath candles with reading (see page 14.)

Congregational Singing: "Let's Get Ready, A Savior's Coming"

Scripture: Matthew 1:18-24 and Luke 1:26-38

Congregational Singing: "Angel Band" (Power Point slides # 11-15)

> Angel Department brings angel ornaments forward.

Scripture: Luke 2:1-7

Congregational Singing: "Away in a Manger"

Manger Department brings manger ornaments forward.

Reading of The Legend of the Candy Cane.

Scripture: Luke 2:8-20

Congregational Singing: "Bethlehem"

> Candy Cane Department brings candy cane ornaments forward.

Scripture: Matthew 2:1-12

Congregational Singing: "We Three Kings"

> Star Department brings star ornaments forward.

Scripture: Luke 2:15-20

Congregational Singing: "Go, Tell It on the Mountain"

> Card Department brings cards forward.

Congregational Singing: "Joy to the World"

> Bakery Department brings baked goods forward.

Benediction: Isaiah 9:2-6

Worship Presentation Outline
CANDY CANE DEPARTMENT

Greeting

Explanation of the chosen mission project and purpose of the sale

Lighting of Advent wreath candles with reading

Congregational Singing: "Let's Get Ready, A Savior's Coming"

Scripture: Matthew 1:18-24 and Luke 1:26-38

Congregational Singing: "Angel Band"

> Angel Department brings angel ornaments forward.

Scripture: Luke 2:1-7

Congregational Singing: "Away in a Manger"

> Manger Department brings manger ornaments forward.

Reading of The Legend of the Candy Cane.

Scripture: Luke 2:8-20

Congregational Singing: "Bethlehem"

Candy Cane Department brings candy cane ornaments forward.

Scripture: Matthew 2:1-12

Congregational Singing: "We Three Kings"

> Star Department brings star ornaments forward.

Scripture: Luke 2:15-20

Congregational Singing: "Go, Tell It on the Mountain"

> Card Department brings cards forward.

Congregational Singing: "Joy to the World"

> Bakery Department brings baked goods forward.

Benediction: Isaiah 9:2-6

The Christmas Shoppe

Worship Presentation Outline
STAR DEPARTMENT

Greeting

Explanation of the chosen mission project and purpose of the sale

Lighting of Advent wreath candles with reading

Congregational Singing: "Let's Get Ready, A Savior's Coming"

Scripture: Matthew 1:18-24 and Luke 1:26-38

Congregational Singing: "Angel Band"

      Angel Department brings angel ornaments forward.

Scripture: Luke 2:1-7

Congregational Singing: "Away in a Manger"

      Manger Department brings manger ornaments forward.

Reading of The Legend of the Candy Cane.

Scripture: Luke 2:8-20

Congregational Singing: "Bethlehem"

      Candy Cane Department brings candy cane ornaments forward.

> **Scripture: Matthew 2:1-12**
>
> **Congregational Singing: "We Three Kings"**
>
> **Star Department brings star ornaments forward.**

Scripture: Luke 2:15-20

Congregational Singing: "Go, Tell It on the Mountain"

      Card Department brings cards forward.

Congregational Singing: "Joy to the World"

      Bakery Department brings baked goods forward.

Benediction: Isaiah 9:2-6

Worship Presentation Outline
CARD DEPARTMENT

Greeting

Explanation of the chosen mission project and purpose of the sale

Lighting of Advent wreath candles with reading

Congregational Singing: "Let's Get Ready, A Savior's Coming"

Scripture: Matthew 1:18-24 and Luke 1:26-38

Congregational Singing: "Angel Band"

> Angel Department brings angel ornaments forward.

Scripture: Luke 2:1-7

Congregational Singing: "Away in a Manger"

> Manger Department brings manger ornaments forward.

Reading of The Legend of the Candy Cane.

Scripture: Luke 2:8-20

Congregational Singing: "Bethlehem"

> Candy Cane Department brings candy cane ornaments forward.

Scripture: Matthew 2:1-12

Congregational Singing: "We Three Kings"

> Star Department brings star ornaments forward.

Scripture: Luke 2:15-20

Congregational Singing: "Go, Tell It on the Mountain"

Card Department brings cards forward.

Congregational Singing: "Joy to the World"

> Bakery Department brings baked goods forward.

Benediction: Isaiah 9:2-6

The Christmas Shoppe

Worship Presentation Outline
BAKERY DEPARTMENT

Greeting

Explanation of the chosen mission project and purpose of the sale

Lighting of Advent wreath candles with reading

Congregational Singing: "Let's Get Ready, A Savior's Coming"

Scripture: Matthew 1:18-24 and Luke 1:26-38

Congregational Singing: "Angel Band"

   Angel Department brings angel ornaments forward.

Scripture: Luke 2:1-7

Congregational Singing: "Away in a Manger"

   Manger Department brings manger ornaments forward.

Reading of The Legend of the Candy Cane.

Scripture: Luke 2:8-20

Congregational Singing: "Bethlehem"

   Candy Cane Department brings candy cane ornaments forward.

Scripture: Matthew 2:1-12

Congregational Singing: "We Three Kings"

   Star Department brings star ornaments forward

Scripture: Luke 2:15-20

Congregational Singing: "Go, Tell It on the Mountain"

   Card Department brings cards forward.

Congregational Singing: "Joy to the World"
Bakery Department brings baked goods forward.

Benediction: Isaiah 9:2-6

Departments Index

Crafts and Baked Goods Index

Patterns Index

A Christmas Shoppe with a real difference!

Leave behind your preconceptions of a Christmas shop as a place to buy things you don't really need. This experience is Christ-centered, and shopping is not the point. *The Christmas Shoppe* is an event where children of all ages will hear the Christmas story, create Christmas symbols to be sold to support a mission project of the church's choice, and prepare and participate in a worship service with parents or with the entire congregation.

The Christmas Shoppe is experienced through six departments:

1. Angel Department
2. Manger Department
3. Candy Department
4. Star Department
5. Card Department
6. Bakery Department

The **CD-ROM** provides music, PowerPoints® , and scripts.

DAPHNA FLEGAL is currently the lead editor for children's curriculum at The United Methodist Publishing House. She is the writer of *Sign & Say Bible Verses for Children*, among other books.

MARCIA STONER is currently an editor of tween curriculum for The United Methodist Publishing House. She is the writer of *What Is Advent?* among other books.

Abingdon Press
www.abingdonpress.com

PQH191832

ISBN-13: 978-1-426-74295-8

90000

9 781426 742958